LL 8/2016

110

D1288694

TODAY'S SUPERSTARS

Miranda Cosgrove

By Autumn Roza and Greg Roza

Gareth Stevens
Publishing

Please visit our Web site, www.garethstevens.com. For a free color catalog of all our high-quality books, call toll free 1-800-542-2595 or fax 1-877-542-2596.

Library of Congress Cataloging-in-Publication Data

Roza, Autumn.
 Miranda Cosgrove / Autumn Roza and Greg Roza.
    p. cm. — (Today's superstars)
 Includes bibliographical references and index.
 ISBN 978-1-4339-3999-0 (pbk.)
 ISBN 978-1-4339-4000-2 (6-pack)
 ISBN 978-1-4339-3998-3 (library binding)
 1. Cosgrove, Miranda, 1993—Juvenile literature. 2. Actors—United States—Biography—Juvenile literature.
 I. Roza, Greg. II. Title.
 PN2287.C634R69 2010
 791.4302'8092—dc22
 [B]

                              2010017400
First Edition

Published in 2011 by
Gareth Stevens Publishing
111 East 14th Street, Suite 349
New York, NY 10003

Copyright © 2011 Gareth Stevens Publishing

Designer: Christopher Logan
Editor: Therese Shea

Photo credits: Cover, p. 1 Brendan Hoffman/Getty Images; p. 4 John Shearer/WireImage/Getty Images; p. 6 Kevin Winter/Getty Images for KCA; pp. 7, 30 Jason Merritt/Film Magic/Getty Images; p. 8 (left) Bobby Bank/FilmMagic/Getty Images; p. 8 (right) Michael Buckner/Getty Images; pp. 9, 12, 22, 24, 25 (top and bottom), 40 Frazer Harrison/Getty Images; p. 10 Mark Mainz/Getty Images; p. 13 Neilson Barnard/Getty Images for Quaker Chewy; p. 14 Jason LaVeris/WireImage/Getty Images; p. 15 Bryan Bedder/Getty Images for Nickelodeon; pp. 16, 18, 20 Frederick M. Brown/Getty Images; p. 19 George Pimentel/WireImage/Getty Images; p. 21 Jeffrey Mayer/WireImage/Getty Images; p. 26 Donald Weber/Getty Images; p. 27 Charley Gallay/WireImage/Getty Images; p. 28 Matthew Peyton/Getty Images for Nickelodeon; p. 31 Frank Micelotta/Getty Images; p. 32 Scott Gries/Getty Images for Nickelodeon; pp. 33, 41 Ben Hider/Getty Images; p. 34 Amy Graves/WireImage/Getty Images; p. 36 Ethan Miller/Getty Images; p. 37 Steve Fenn/ABC via Getty Images; p. 38 Todd Williamson/WireImage/Getty Images; p. 39 Marcel Thomas/Film Magic/Getty Images; p. 46 Joe Kohen/WireImage/Getty Images.

All rights reserved. No part of this book may be reproduced in any form without permission in writing from the publisher, except by a reviewer.

Printed in the United States of America

CPSIA compliance information: Batch #CS10GS: For further information contact Gareth Stevens, New York, New York at 1-800-542-2595.

Contents

Words in the glossary appear in **bold** type the first time they are used in the text.

"She's just a girl. She's beautiful and cool, AND SHE COULD ALSO BE YOUR BEST FRIEND."

—Dan Schneider, creator of *iCarly*

Cosgrove strikes a pose on March 27, 2010, at the 23rd annual Kids' Choice Awards.

Chapter 1

Top Teen Star

The fifty-fourth **episode** of *iCarly*, titled "iSaved Your Life," caused a stir among fans even before it aired. Rumor had it that two of the show's stars—Miranda Cosgrove and Nathan Kress—were going to share a long-awaited kiss! Their characters, Carly Shay and Freddie Benson, were best friends, but many fans thought they'd make a great couple.

"iSaved Your Life" was a high point in Cosgrove's television career. The episode set a record for the number of viewers of a live-action show on the Nickelodeon television network. Cosgrove is quickly becoming one of America's favorite actors, but she's not a newcomer to entertainment. She's appeared in numerous movies, shows, and commercials.

Show Time!

iCarly is about three friends in Seattle, Washington, who create a Web show. Meanwhile, they get into a lot of crazy situations in real life!

Carly and her friend Sam perform funny skits and weird stunts for their online show. They also show silly videos that viewers send them. Many of these videos come from real iCarly fans! Cosgrove explains, "It's a show within a show because fans send in tapes and we show [them] on air."

Fact File

Carly and Spencer's father doesn't appear on iCarly. He's in the U.S. Navy.

Meet the Cast

Besides Carly, iCarly has three other main characters. Jennette McCurdy (above, second from left) plays Carly's partner and best friend, Sam Puckett, a bossy yet loveable teen. Nathan Kress (above, second from right) plays Freddie the show's technology expert and cameraman. Together, Carly, Sam, and Freddie help make the Web show iCarly a success. Jerry Trainor (above, at left) plays Carly's brother, Spencer, her legal guardian and an artist. He's constantl clowning around, which keeps the audience laughing.

"iSaved Your Life"

At the beginning of "iSaved Your Life," Sam runs in to tell Spencer some news. Freddie was hit by a taco truck after pushing Carly out of its way. Sam is actually eating a taco as she talks to Spencer! Freddie is badly injured, and Carly considers him a hero. She tries to take care of him. At one point, Freddie falls down in the shower and Carly has to help him. She puts goggles stuffed with socks on her eyes so she won't see him naked!

As with every episode of *iCarly*, there's much more going on. The main characters are also involved in a paintball war they call "assassin"!

TRUE OR FALSE?

On *iCarly*, Freddie's real name is Fredward.

For answers, see page 46.

The main characters of *iCarly* often make appearances together.

Number One!

The **premiere** of "iSaved Your Life" on January 18, 2010, was more than a success—it topped the broadcast ratings for all programs that aired in its time slot. This included very popular shows, such as the Fox network drama 24. A total of 12.4 million viewers tuned in to see Carly and Freddie's first kiss! This makes it the most watched live-action show Nickelodeon has ever aired.

Fact File

Cosgrove presented the award for Best Group at the 2009 MTV Europe Music Video Awards in Berlin, Germany. The winner was a German band named Tokio Hotel.

Miranda's Favorites

✔ **Movies:** *Mean Girls, The Notebook,* and *To Kill a Mockingbird*

✔ **TV shows:** *Gilmore Girls, The Secret Life of the American Teenager*

✔ **Musicians:** Gwen Stefani, Avril Lavigne, and Paramore

✔ **Color:** Purple

✔ **Food:** Cupcakes

✔ **Fashion:** **Vintage** clothing

Cosgrove enjoys meeting her fans and signing autographs.

Star Power

The success of "iSaved Your Life" helped convince Nickelodeon to bring *iCarly* back for a fourth season. Many reports said that Cosgrove would be earning around $180,000 per episode. The fourth season is a total of 26 episodes! That's more money than many popular adult actors make today.

Cosgrove is used to fame. She's been acting since she was 4 years old! Her natural talent has earned her acting jobs in commercials, television shows, and movies. She's just starting a career in music. The show *iCarly* has also been used as a basis for books and video games!

TRUE OR FALSE?

At the 2010 Nickelodeon Kids' Choice Awards, Cosgrove presented an award to President Barack Obama.

On January 23, 2010, Cosgrove attended the Screen Actors Guild Award Ceremony in Los Angeles, California.

"I was singing and dancing and playing around, AND A LADY ASKED MY MOM IF I WANTED TO JOIN HER AGENCY."
—Miranda Cosgrove

Cosgrove attends a showing of *The Ant Bully* in 2006.

Chapter 2
Natural Talent

On May 14, 1993, Miranda Taylor Cosgrove was born in Los Angeles, California. Her parents, Tom and Chris, owned a dry-cleaning business. Although she's an only child, Cosgrove always had many friends. She's still close to her childhood friends.

Cosgrove has always been outgoing, and she has always loved performing. When she was just 3 years old, Cosgrove was at a restaurant with her family. She was dancing and singing songs from the movie *Grease* when a woman came over and introduced herself. It turned out that she was a **talent scout**. She knew the little girl had what it takes to make it in show business.

Getting Started

Cosgrove's first **audition** led to her first acting job in a Mello Yello soda commercial when she was just 4 years old. The commercial took place on a beach. According to Cosgrove, the crew had spent a lot of time building a sand castle. It was supposed to look like she was building it, but she kicked it over instead! "I guess I wasn't good at taking direction," Cosgrove said.

TRUE OR FALSE?
In second grade, Cosgrove auditioned to be an astronaut in a school play.

All About Miranda

Birth date: May 14, 1993

Birthplace: Los Angeles, California

Parents: Tom and Chris Cosgrove

Right– or left–handed: Left-handed

Hobbies: Horseback riding and **fencing**

▼ Cosgrove poses with the cast members of the hit show *Drake & Josh*.

That's Entertainment

When Cosgrove isn't working on *iCarly*, she enjoys searching entertainment Web sites such as YouTube for interesting, funny, or strange videos. Sometimes she finds videos that appear on her television show.

During season 2, Internet star Lucas Cruikshank—better known as Fred—appeared on an episode of *iCarly*. Cosgrove discovered Lucas while watching his crazy videos on YouTube!

Going Full-Time

The Mello Yello soda commercial was just the start of Cosgrove's acting career. Soon after, she appeared in Burger King and McDonald's commercials. She also landed several modeling jobs for well-known businesses, including *Bon Appetit* magazine and Kmart.

By the time she was 7, Cosgrove had decided she wanted to be a full-time actor. She began auditioning for parts in plays and television shows. Cosgrove was about to become a big star.

Fact File

Miranda's mom has nicknames for her. She calls her Randall and sometimes Randy. Miranda thinks these names are embarrassing!

What About School?

After completing fifth grade, Cosgrove began to be homeschooled to allow her to concentrate on acting and music. In addition to homeschooling, a tutor helps Cosgrove study and prepare for tests when she's at work.

In 2009, Cosgrove was **inducted** into the National Honor Society. She doesn't make a big deal about it though. "My mom is all excited about it, but I thought it was a rip-off because all I got was a pin."

TRUE OR FALSE?

In addition to being homeschooled, Cosgrove has participated in online school courses.

What Is the National Honor Society?

Established in 1921, the National Honor Society (NHS) recognizes the achievements of outstanding high school students across the nation. This organization is managed by the National Association of Secondary School Principals (NASSP). The NASSP awards NHS membership to high school students who have shown promise in the areas of scholarship, leadership, service, and character.

College Plans

For Cosgrove, college is an important part of her plans after high school. "I definitely want to go to college," Cosgrove said. "That's a big thing with me . . . I'd love to be an actor, but I'd also like to be a marine biologist. I'm really into the sea."

Where does Cosgrove hope to go to college? Her parents would like her to attend the University of Southern California, which is where her father went. It's also not too far from home. However, Cosgrove loves New York City. She's considering New York University. Cosgrove hopes her college plans will include several of her close friends.

Fact File

Cosgrove has a bike with two seats. She says her friends let her do all the pedaling!

Always happy to meet fans, Cosgrove takes time to sign autographs during a Nickelodeon event in New York City on March 11, 2010.

"It was really amazing getting to work with Jack Black.

I WAS REALLY LUCKY."

—Miranda Cosgrove

The *School of Rock* cast pose for a group photo on September 24, 2003.

Chapter 3

Big Break

In 2001, when Cosgrove was just 7 years old, she got her first big break in television acting—except she didn't actually appear on screen! She was chosen to do the voice part of a young Lana Lang for the **pilot** of the television show *Smallville*. An actor named Jade Unterman played Lana Lang as a young girl. Unterman pretended to be a fairy princess, but the voice was Miranda's.

Cosgrove's first big break in the movies came in 2002. She was very busy auditioning for television shows and movies at this time. She auditioned for a part in the 2003 movie *School of Rock*, starring actor Jack Black. Out of hundreds of actors, Cosgrove got the part of Summer Hathaway!

TRUE OR FALSE?

The role of Summer Hathaway was Cosgrove's first acting part in a movie.

School of Rock

School of Rock is about an out-of-work musician named Dewey Finn, played by Jack Black. His mission in the movie is to turn a bunch of private school students into a rock band. Cosgrove plays a bright, sassy student named Summer Hathaway. She's the classic teacher's pet! Although Summer doesn't get to sing in the band, Finn chooses her to be the band's manager.

After an exciting "battle of the bands," the kids help Finn open his own "school of rock." Cosgrove's last scene shows Summer Hathaway setting up a record deal over the phone!

WE DON'T NEED NO EDUCATION

School of Rock

MR. BLACK
ACCEPT NO SUBSTITUTES

Cosgrove and the rest of the kids in the cast learned that Jack Black loves to joke around.

The Kids of *School of Rock*

The *School of Rock* "students" were selected by the movie's director and writer after a nationwide talent search. All of them were skilled musicians. At 10 years old, Cosgrove was the youngest of the child actors. Rebecca Brown learned to play bass for the movie. Joey Gaydos Jr. played lead guitar. The keyboard player was Robert Tsai. Kevin Clark—the oldest of the group at 14—played the drums. With Jack Black as lead singer, the group put on a great show!

Box Office Hit

School of Rock did very well at the **box office**. It earned more than $19 million for its opening weekend, making it the number-one movie in the United States! As of 2010, the movie had earned over $131 million worldwide. It also won several awards, including Best Family Feature Film at the 2004 Young Artist Awards. As part of a family comedy favorite, Cosgrove made her mark in the acting world.

Fact File

Cosgrove began taking singing lessons when she was 5. However, her character in *School of Rock* was a bad singer. She had to learn how to sing badly for her role!

Rising Star

School of Rock showcased the musical talents of its young actors. Even though Cosgrove didn't play a musician in the movie, her popularity grew more than that of the other young actors. Jack Black was already a big star, but Cosgrove stood out, too. She proved she could make it in show business.

Cosgrove's role in *School of Rock* helped reinforce her passion for music. She said, "After making the movie, I went home and got out all [my mom's] old albums and listened to them." She especially liked the Rolling Stones!

Fact File

Cosgrove has voiced characters for several cartoons, including an episode of *What's New, Scooby-Doo?* She also voiced a mouse named Munch in the 2005 movie *Here Comes Peter Cottontail.*

▼ The cast of *School of Rock* pose for a photo with Sherry Lansing of Paramount Pictures movie studio.

Miranda in Demand-a!

Cosgrove's role in *School of Rock* helped her land more acting jobs. She earned several small television parts. In 2004, she appeared on the **sitcom** *Grounded for Life*. Cosgrove also appeared in more movies. She played Joni North in the 2005 movie *Yours, Mine and Ours*. In 2006, she played Karen Sussman in *Keeping Up with the Steins*.

While Cosgrove was working on *School of Rock*, she learned that she was going to play a major role in a new television show on the kids' cable network Nickelodeon. It would be the part that truly launched her career.

Cosgrove poses for a photo at the premiere of *Yours, Mine and Ours*.

TRUE OR FALSE?

Cosgrove was 10 years old when she auditioned for a part on *Drake & Josh*.

21

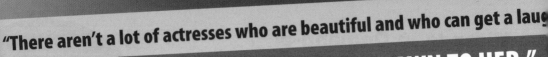

"There aren't a lot of actresses who are beautiful and who can get a laug

EVERYONE IS REALLY DRAWN TO HER."

—Paula Kaplan, Nickelodeon talent executive

NICKELODEON®

The *Drake & Josh* cast pose with their 2006 Kids' Choice Award for Favorite TV Show.

Chapter 4
Sitcom Star

While Cosgrove was working on *School of Rock*, she auditioned for a role in a new sitcom on the Nickelodeon television network—*Drake & Josh*. She wanted the role of Megan Parker, the younger sister of Drake and Josh. She got the job! Cosgrove was very enthusiastic about her first regular part in a sitcom.

Drake Bell, who played Drake Parker, remembers first meeting Cosgrove when the show was just in the planning stages. "We were walking to the writers' room, and I remember hearing the pitter-patter of these little feet behind me. She was just standing there saying, 'So where are we going? What are we doing?' I thought, 'Well, this is going to be fun.' " And it was!

Drake and Josh

In the show, Drake Parker and Josh Nichols (played by Josh Peck) are teenage stepbrothers who live in San Diego, California. Drake is lucky, talented, and popular. He's also careless and lazy. Josh is responsible and smart, but also **sarcastic** and unlucky. He usually gets into trouble when Drake's plans backfire.

Drake and Josh deal with everyday teen issues, such as school and dating. They also have to deal with their spoiled, mean little sister Megan.

Fact File

The pilot for *Drake & Josh* first aired on January 11, 2004.

Who Is Josh Peck?

Joshua Michael "Josh" Peck was born on November 10, 1986, in New York City. When he was just 8 years old, he got his start in entertainment as a stand-up comedian! He's appeared in numerous movies and television shows. After appearing on the Nickelodeon **sketch comedy** program *The Amanda Show*, Josh was selected to star in his own sitcom. You might know Josh as the voice of Eddie, the opossum from the *Ice Age* movies. Josh also likes to play piano and hockey.

Megan

Cosgrove plays Megan. The character loves playing pranks on Drake and Josh, but she seems never to get caught by her parents. Usually, the boys get into trouble instead. "Megan drives them crazy with her pranks," Cosgrove said about Megan. "She even drenches them from head-to-toe with paint. I'd never do anything like that."

Cosgrove poses here with Ashley Argota from the show *True Jackson, VP.*

TRUE OR FALSE?

On *Drake & Josh*, Megan hired a little boy named Tyler to help prank her older brothers.

Who Is Drake Bell?

Jared Drake Bell, known as Drake Bell, was born on June 27, 1986, in Santa Ana, California. Drake has appeared in many commercials, sitcoms, and movies. He was also an actor on *The Amanda Show* before starring in *Drake & Josh*. Josh has been singing and playing the guitar since 2001. He even recorded the theme song for *Drake & Josh*. He's released two solo albums and is working on a third.

Sitcom Success

Drake & Josh became a big hit with kids and parents alike. The premiere show earned the highest ratings for a Nickelodeon live-action show in nearly 10 years. The chemistry between Drake and Josh helped the show achieve its popularity. They really seemed like brothers—hilarious brothers! Cosgrove stood out, too, and played a big part in creating a following for the show.

Some people are surprised that Cosgrove could play a role like Megan Parker. Megan is as mean and cruel as Miranda is sweet and likeable. "I don't think I've seen [Cosgrove] in a bad mood once in my life," said the show's creator, Dan Schneider. It's a glowing credit to Cosgrove's ability as an actor that she can play someone so different from herself.

Fact File

Cosgrove performs many of her own stunts on *iCarly*.

Cosgrove attends a screening of *School of Rock* in Toronto, Canada, in September 2003.

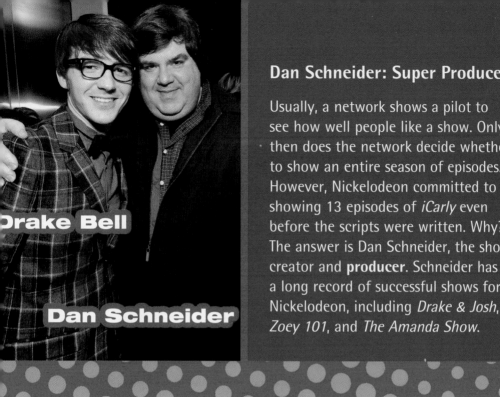

Drake Bell

Dan Schneider

Dan Schneider: Super Producer!

Usually, a network shows a pilot to see how well people like a show. Only then does the network decide whether to show an entire season of episodes. However, Nickelodeon committed to showing 13 episodes of *iCarly* even before the scripts were written. Why? The answer is Dan Schneider, the show's creator and **producer**. Schneider has a long record of successful shows for Nickelodeon, including *Drake & Josh*, *Zoey 101*, and *The Amanda Show*.

Moving On

Drake & Josh ran for four seasons. After that, the cast got back together to make several specials. Even though *Drake & Josh* was approaching the end, Dan Schneider had plans for Cosgrove. He knew her talent and personality would be perfect for a new show he had in mind.

Drake, Josh, and Miranda have remained great friends. Her "older brothers" helped her gain the confidence she needed to star in her own show.

TRUE OR FALSE?

Cosgrove has guest-starred on the show *Hannah Montana*.

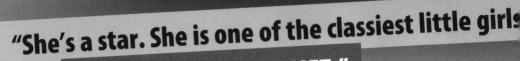

"She's a star. She is one of the classiest little girls
THAT I'VE EVER MET."

—Dan Schneider, creator of *iCarly*

Cosgrove poses for
a photo with a copy
of *iCarly: Music from
and Inspired by the
Hit TV Show.*

Chapter 5

iCarly

In 2007, Cosgrove began starring in her own television show. *iCarly* is about a young teenager, her two pals, and their online Web show. Carly Shay and her friends film humorous skits in her home. Their Web show also features wild videos sent in by real *iCarly* viewers. When Carly isn't starring in her Web show, she and her friends are involved with equally funny adventures.

Fans of the show know that *iCarly* is at times crazy, goofy, and hilarious. The humor and laugh-out-loud scenes are part of what keeps fans interested. It's also fun for the cast. "Filming an episode is really fast-paced," said Cosgrove. "We're always running, changing, and putting on crazy costumes."

How'd It All Start?

Why do Carly and her friends have a Web show? It's a funny story from the first episode.

Fact File

One of the first videos on *iCarly* showed a boy who could suck milk into his nose and squirt it out his eye!

Sam posts photos of a rhinoceros around the school — with her least favorite teacher's head on it. Carly takes the blame. Her punishment is to hold auditions for the school talent show. Freddie, who has a crush on Carly, agrees to film the auditions. However, the talent acts they pick for the show are rejected by school officials.

Carly, Sam, and Freddie decide to post their favorite auditions online. The video becomes a huge hit. Soon after, the trio start their own Web show.

The cast of *iCarly* pose for a photo with Dan Schneider, the show's creator and producer.

Weird Stuff!

    iCarly stands out from other shows. It's based in part on Internet videos sent in by real people. In fact, the "i" in "iCarly" stands for "Internet." Although the episodes focus on events in Carly Shay's life, they always feature odd and often senseless skits and jokes. And fans seem to love it. "I go online a lot," said Dan Schneider, "and I read stuff all the time from fans saying they love the weird stuff, the stuff that doesn't belong anywhere or make any sense."

TRUE OR FALSE?

Cosgrove likes to show people her own silly trick. She can make her eyes wiggle.

You Can Be a Star, Too!

Anyone can send their own crazy videos to the *iCarly* show. It might even be used on the show! The *iCarly* Web site has videos of the stars telling viewers how to make a video that might be featured on the show.

Also included on the Web site are questions for fans to answer about their likes and dislikes. There are even *iCarly* games to play!

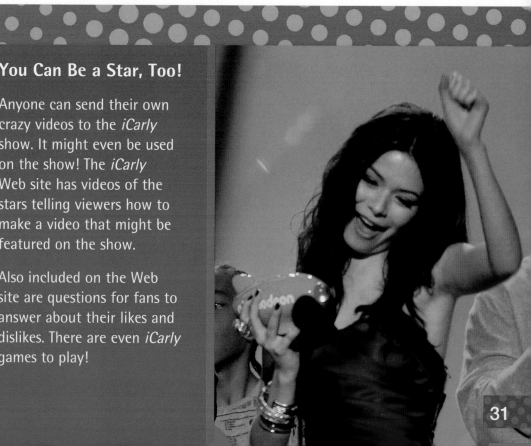

Who Is Kelly Cooper?

One popular skit from *iCarly* has become a hit with fans on the Internet. It pokes fun at many movies that have been made for young audiences. *Kelly Cooper: Terrible Movie* is a fake movie trailer about a girl named Kelly (played by Carly) who wants to fit in with the cool kids at school. She also seems to fall down a lot for no apparent reason. The announcer in the trailer claims the movie is "a comedy that no one wants to see!"

Fact File

iCarly has featured numerous guest stars, including *American Idol* star David Archuleta and the bands the Plain White T's and Good Charlotte.

Until Next Time . . .

Whether they're shaving stuffed animals or making bacon puppets, Carly and Sam know how to make the fans of their Web show laugh. It's complete craziness from beginning to end! Even the way they say goodbye is comical—as in this example from the episode "iMeet Fred."

Carly: Until next time, stay in school,

Sam: recycle,

Carly: pour milk on your parents,

Sam: hug a duck,

Carly: eat a stick of butter,

Sam: and shampoo a squirrel, goodbye!

The New Champ

In spring 2009, *iCarly* passed the reigning champion of kids' television, *Hannah Montana*, in the ratings for young audiences. This was a huge milestone for the rising star. In fact, the second season of *iCarly* was the number-one series for kids aged 2 to 14, with an average television audience of 5.6 million viewers.

Cosgrove's success in television has helped her gain an audience for her music career.

"Leave It All to Me"

Cosgrove doesn't only star in *iCarly*—she sings the theme song! She performs the song called "Leave It All to Me" with her former costar Drake Bell. In 2008, Sony Music released an album called *iCarly: Music from and Inspired by the Hit TV Show*. The album contains funny lines from the show and hits from music stars such as Good Charlotte and Avril Lavigne. It also features three songs performed by Cosgrove—"Stay My Baby," "About You Now," and "Headphones On."

TRUE OR FALSE?

In 2009, Cosgrove hosted a 2-hour show called *MTV Teen Cribs*.

"It's just such a good feeling

TO KNOW PEOPLE ARE ACTUALLY WATCHING."

—Miranda Cosgrove

Cosgrove signs autographs at Bloomingdale's in Costa Mesa, California, on August 25, 2008.

Chapter 6
What's Next, Miranda?

On March 27, 2010, Cosgrove and the other actors on *iCarly* won the Nickelodeon Kids' Choice Award for Favorite TV Show. Cosgrove is quickly becoming a superstar! Filming for the fourth season of *iCarly* began in spring 2010.

While Cosgrove will continue making *iCarly*, she's also branching out. In 2009, she appeared in the movie *The Wild Stallion*. The story was a perfect fit for Cosgrove because she loves horses.

She also returned to voice acting in the 2010 **animated** movie *Despicable Me*. She plays an orphan named Margo. Cosgrove performs with comedian Steve Carell, who plays the evil villain that Margo would like to be her dad!

TRUE OR FALSE?

Cosgrove recorded a song for the 2009 movie *Monsters vs. Aliens*.

Music Career

Now that Cosgrove has established herself as an actor, she's been spending more time working on her singing career. Although she's been singing for many years, recording music is still a new venture for her. "I've been singing since I was little, but now I'm making a CD and writing songs. I never imagined I'd get to do any of it," she said.

Cosgrove released her first album in April 2010. It's called *Sparks Fly*. The first music video for a song from the album, "Kissin' U," premiered on March 19 during the *iCarly* special "iFix a Pop Star."

Cosgrove's love of singing comes out in her performances.

Cosgrove makes time for a young fan in Las Vegas, Nevada.

Beauty Ambassador

In February 2010, Cosgrove was asked to become the newest "Brand **Ambassador**" for Neutrogena, a beauty product company. Other famous women who have held this title in the past include actors Jennifer Garner, Vanessa Hudgens, and Emma Roberts. Neutrogena president Jim Colleran said, "Miranda **embodies** the youthful and vibrant spirit that has always been part of the Neutrogena brand. We are proud to have her as our newest ambassador."

Fact File

Cosgrove has appeared on several talk shows, including the *Today Show*, *The Ellen DeGeneres Show*, and *Rachael Ray*.

By the Numbers

4 Age when Cosgrove started acting

16 Age when Cosgrove released her first album, *Sparks Fly*

96 Total number of *iCarly* episodes after four seasons

12.4 million Number of people who watched *iCarly* on January 18, 2010

Giving Back

Not only is Cosgrove known for her acting and singing, she's also known for participating in charitable activities. On July 28, 2009, Cosgrove joined other young stars, such as the Jonas Brothers, in visiting St. Jude's Hospital in Memphis, Tennessee. Cosgrove met sick children, played games with them, and helped raise money for the hospital. She's also participated in a program called Math-a-Thon that helps kids from kindergarten through eighth grade improve their math skills.

Fact File

In April 2009, Cosgrove worked with Explore-A-Story, a Los Angeles reading program. She read the book *Dear Mrs. LaRue: Letters from Obedience School* to elementary school children.

A Celebration o

Miranda Grants a Wish

In 2009, Cosgrove attended a celebration in Los Angeles for the Make-A-Wish Foundation's fifth annual Season of Wishes. She met with Ana De la Canal, a 6-year-old Texas girl with a life-threatening illness. What was Ana's wish? To meet her favorite TV star, Miranda Cosgrove! Cosgrove made a little girl's wish come true.

Miranda on the Rise

Cosgrove's charitable and professional life continue to be busy. In 2010, she teamed up with Quaker Oats and the Afterschool Alliance to help promote after-school programs for kids all over the country. The Afterschool Alliance is a major supporter of quality, affordable after-school activities in the nation. Thanks to Cosgrove, the Quaker Oats company was able to provide resources for 26,000 programs. Cosgrove also performed a special concert for one lucky contest winner and their friends!

TRUE OR FALSE?

Cosgrove performed the song "Kissin' U" at the Macy's Thanksgiving Day Parade in 2008.

Miranda's popularity continues to rise. She's a talented actor and singer, but she's also a dedicated student and a generous human being. Whatever Miranda chooses to do, she's sure to be a huge success.

Cosgrove waves from the Build-a-Bear Float during the 2008 Macy's Thanksgiving Day Parade in New York City.

Timeline

1993   Cosgrove is born on May 14 in Los Angeles, California.

2001   Cosgrove gets her first job on a television show.

2003   Cosgrove appears as Summer Hathaway in the movie *School of Rock*.

2004   Cosgrove first appears as Megan Parker on *Drake & Josh*.

2007   Cosgrove begins playing Carly Shay on *iCarly*.

Cosgrove and actor Lily Collins attend a party after the premiere of "Merry Christmas, Drake & Josh."

2008 Sony Music releases the album *iCarly: Music from and Inspired by the Hit TV Show.*

2009 Cosgrove's song "Raining Sunshine" is featured in the movie *Cloudy with a Chance of Meatballs.*

2010 The *iCarly* episode "iSaved Your Life" is viewed by 12.4 million people.

2010 Cosgrove becomes an ambassador for Neutrogena.

2010 Cosgrove releases her first album, *Sparks Fly.*

Glossary

ambassador: someone who serves as an official representative for something

animated: consisting of drawings or computer images that appear to move

audition: a test taken by an actor who is trying to get a role

box office: a place where movie tickets are sold, or the overall sale of tickets for a movie

embody: to give a form to an idea

episode: one show in a television series

fencing: the art or sport of fighting with slim, bendable swords

induct: to admit someone into a society or group

pilot: the first show of a television series, often used by television networks to see if people will like the show

premiere: a performance shown to the public for the first time

producer: someone who organizes and supervises the making of a television show, movie, or play

sarcastic: speaking in a manner that sounds bitter or mean, but is often meant to be humorous

sitcom: a humorous television show based on events that could happen in real life. Short for "situation comedy."

sketch comedy: a show featuring short, humorous skits, which are often unrelated to each other

talent scout: someone hired to find talented people, especially in entertainment and sports

vintage: something from the past, especially something that is still considered valuable or fashionable

To Find Out More

Books

Corse, Nicole, and Dan Schneider. *iCarly: Official Scrapbook.*
  New York, NY: Scholastic Inc., 2009.

Leaveitt, Aime Jane. *Miranda Cosgrove.* Hockessin, DE:
  Mitchell Lane Publishers, 2009.

Ryals, Lexi. *Miranda Mania: An Unauthorized Biography.*
  New York, NY: Price Stern Sloan, 2008.

Spencer, Liv. *The Miranda Cosgrove and iCarly Spectacular!
  Unofficial and Unstoppable.* Toronto, ON, Canada:
  ECW Press, 2010.

Web Sites

iCarly.com
www.icarly.com
Find out what's new on *iCarly* and watch videos from the
show. Also, find out how you can submit videos.

Miranda Cosgrove
www.mirandacosgroveofficial.com
Find out all the latest news about Miranda on her official Web site.

Miranda Cosgrove Online
www.mirandaonline.org
Read the news and facts about Miranda on this fan-based Web site.

Nick
www.nick.com
Explore media related to all of the Nickelodeon network's
shows, including *iCarly.*

Publisher's note to educators and parents: Our editors have carefully reviewed these Web sites to ensure that they are suitable for students. Many Web sites change frequently, however, and we cannot guarantee that a site's future contents will continue to meet our high standards of quality and educational value. Be advised that students should be closely supervised whenever they access the Internet.

Major Awards

Young Artist Awards

2004 Best Family Feature Film—Comedy or Musical
(School of Rock)

2009 Best Performance in a TV Series
(Comedy or Drama)—Leading Young Actress

Australian Nickelodeon Kids' Choice Awards

2009 Favorite Comedy Show *(iCarly)*

Nickelodeon Kids' Choice Awards

2006 Favorite TV Show *(Drake & Josh)*

2008 Favorite TV Show *(Drake & Josh)*

2009 Favorite TV Show *(iCarly)*

2010 Favorite TV Show *(iCarly)*

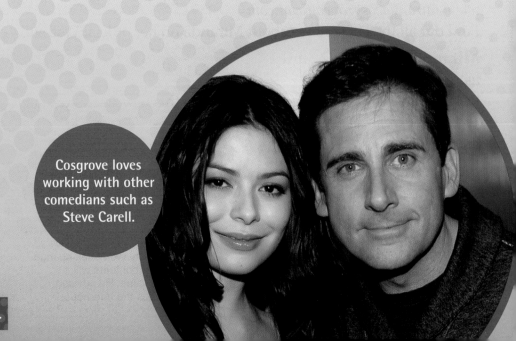

Cosgrove loves working with other comedians such as Steve Carell.

Source Notes

p. 4 Denise Martin, "Ruler of the Tweens," *Los Angeles Times*, April 28, 2009, http://articles.latimes.com/2009/apr/28/entertainment/et-icarly28.

p. 6 "Miranda Cosgrove," Yahoo! Movies, http://movies.yahoo.com/movie/contributor/1808514316/bio (accessed March 30, 2010).

p. 10 Betsy Boyd, "Up Next: Miranda Cosgrove," *Variety*, October 4, 2007, http://www.variety.com/article/VR1117973328.html?categoryid=2721&cs=1.

p. 12 "Miranda Cosgrove: Lets Loose!" *People*, October 14, 2009, http://www.people.com/people/archive/article/0,,20306321,00.html.

p. 14 "The Making of Miranda," *People*, October 14, 2009, http://www.people.com/people/archive/article/0,,20306320,00.html.

p. 15 "Miranda Cosgrove Biography," Kidzworld, http://www.kidzworld.com/article/12806-miranda-cosgrove-biography (accessed March 30, 2010).

p. 16 "About to Pop: Miranda Cosgrove," PopEater, http://www.popeater.com/2008/12/18/about-to-pop-miranda-cosgrove (accessed March 30, 2010).

p. 20 Ethan Aames, "Interview: The Kids of 'School of Rock'!" Cinema Confidential, October 1, 2003, http://www.cinecon.com/news.php?id=0310012.

p. 22 Lisa Ingrassia, "Miranda Cosgrove," *People*, July 28, 2008, http://www.people.com/people/archive/article/0,,20214041,00.html.

p. 23 Jacque Steinberg, "I, Little Sister, Becomes 'iCarly,' " *New York Times*, September 7, 2007, http://www.nytimes.com/2007/09/07/arts/television/07icar.html.

p. 25 "Megan Parker," Nick, http://www.nick.com/shows/drake-and-josh/characters/megan-parker.html (accessed March 30, 2010).

p. 26 Jonathan Dee, "Tween on the Screen," *New York Times*, April 8, 2007, http://www.nytimes.com/2010/03/26/arts/television/26victor.html.

p. 28 Dee.

p. 29 "Behind the Scenes," *People*, October 14, 2009, http://www.people.com/people/archive/article/0,,20306315,00.html.

p. 31 Martin.

p. 32 *iCarly*, season 2, episode 10: "iMeet Fred."

p. 34 Danielle Beavers, "Miranda Cosgrove Plans Solo Album After Conquering TV and Web With 'iCarly'," MTV, July 24, 2008, http://www.mtv.com/news/articles/1591500/20080724/cosgrove__miranda.jhtml.

p. 36 Martin.

p. 37 Jen Garcia, "Miranda Cosgrove Is Neutrogena's Newest Face!" *People*, February 10, 2010, http://stylenews.peoplestylewatch.com/2010/02/11/exclusive-miranda-cosgrove-is-neutrogenas-newest-face/.

True or False Answers

Page 7   True.

Page 9   False. She gave the Big Help Award to First Lady Michelle Obama for her "Let's Move" campaign, which encourages kids to eat right and exercise.

Page 12   False. She auditioned for the part of an alien. She didn't get it.

Page 14   True.

Page 18   True.

Page 21   False. Miranda was just 8 when she auditioned for a part on *Drake & Josh*.

Page 25   True.

Page 27   False. She guest-starred on the shows *Zoey 101* and *Unfabulous* while she was a cast member of *Drake & Josh*.

Page 31   True.

Page 33   True.

Page 36   False. She recorded a song titled "Raining Sunshine" for the 2009 movie *Cloudy with a Chance of Meatballs*.

Page 39   False. She performed "About You Now."

Index

About the Author

Autumn Roza and Greg Roza Autumn is a ten-year-old girl who loves *iCarly* and *Drake & Josh*. When she's not playing with her best friend Johanna (or watching *iCarly*), Autumn is usually reading a *Harry Potter* book. She also enjoys singing, playing violin, and karate.

Greg has been writing and editing kids' books for ten years. He has a master's degree in English from the State University of New York at Fredonia. Greg lives in Hamburg, New York, with his wife and three children. He also enjoys karate and watching *iCarly*!